GW01339138

Before coming to Kilmeston, Ann lived in a variety of places, including Vienna, London, Berlin, Paris, Rome and Washington DC. She met her Scots Guards husband while working for the Foreign Office in Cold-War Berlin and has since tackled a number of ventures, from private German tutor, via watercolour agent, company MD and cryptic crossword compiler, to her latest as an author. Her children and varied musical activities have helped provide a thread of continuity in a roving life-style.

This book is dedicated to:
Olivia, Julian & Stephanie,
with love

Copyright © Ann Smart 1995

Published by Ann Smart 1995

Designed and printed by A3 Litho Ltd Farnham

Colour photographs by Ann Smart

All rights reserved. No part of this publication may be reproduced, stored in a retrieval system, or transmitted, in any form or by any means, electronic, mechanical, photocopying, recording or otherwise, without the prior permission of the publishers.

ISBN 0 9526282 1 X   Paperback Edition

PORTRAIT OF KILMESTON

by
Ann Smart

interlace dry facts with anecdotal "bonnes bouches", so as to aid digestion and enhance pleasure. I hope that those who know little or nothing of Kilmeston may be enchanted by its treasures and that those who know the village already will derive pleasure from discovering even more in these pages.

AMS
1995

PORTRAIT OF KILMESTON

"Far from the madding crowd's ignoble strife"

Most reference books, if they mention Kilmeston at all, merely allude to the source of the River Itchen lying at the bottom of the hill. One describes Kilmeston in little more than a sentence as "...enchanting but for its overhead power cables". Another is more romantic: "Kilmeston ...is a tiny and picturesque village. It has a manor house, a village green, brick-and-tile or pink washed houses, dovecots and clipped yews - all in a picture-book village pattern". All rather standard stuff; but probe a little deeper and a mine of more enticing material emerges...

* * * * *

To go back to somewhere nearer the beginning, Cenelmestun, Cylmestuna, Chelmestune and Culmestone were a few of Kilmeston's earlier names. The land once belonged to the Cathedral Church of Winchester, and records show that in AD 961 King Edgar - under licence from Bishop Brethelm (or Brikthelm) of Winchester - gave the manor and land at Kilmeston to Athelwulf for three generations, the land thereafter to return to the Bishop. At the time of the Domesday survey, ordered by King William I in 1084, it appears to have been known as Chenelmestune.

The land that was given to Athelwulf was divided and formed into two manors. These became known as Kilmeston Plunkenet and Kilmeston Gymme, taking their names from those who then held them. After many changes of ownership - including that of John Tichborne of nearby Tichborne Park - both manors were sold by Henry Lacey in 1739 to George Ridge.

This has swiftly brought us to a key period in Kilmeston's history, when the Ridge family lived at Kilmeston Manor, and one to which we will turn more fully later on.

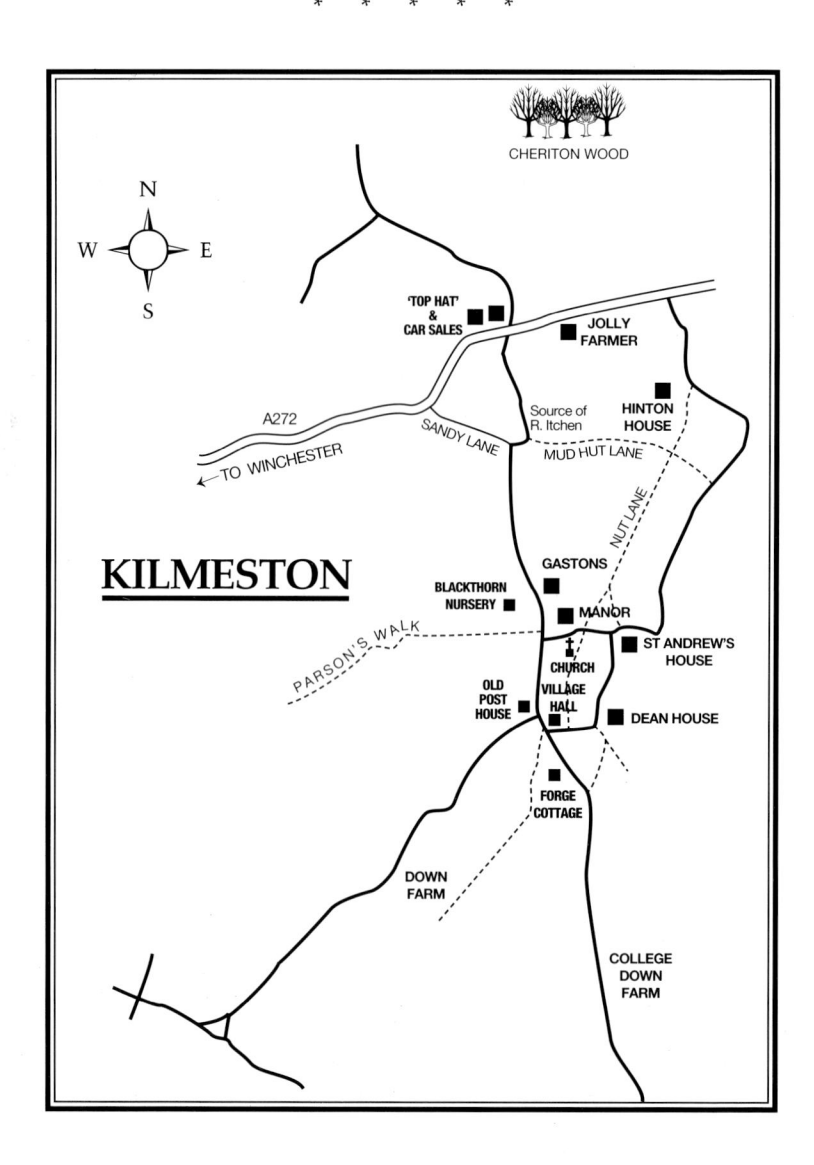

* * * * *

Researchers into local history are customarily drawn first to the church records, but all too often they are floored at the first hurdle, when they arrive to find the church door locked, and most have to be content with what they can discover among the gravestones. At Kilmeston, luckier visitors arrive at a time when Ray Griffen is tending the churchyard or when occupants of the Manor happen to be in their garden and notice strangers trying the church door. Sonia and Jim Passingham from Cowplain were, after numerous ancestry-tracking expeditions elsewhere, finally successful in Kilmeston. Sonia subsequently wrote a warm, friendly and perceptive article about Kilmeston in her parish magazine in March 1993, extracts from which she has generously allowed to be quoted:

> *At the end of November last year we decided to revisit some of the old parishes, now so familiar from our research. We knew that some of the burials had been at Kilmeston, previously in the parish of Cheriton, and one of the most useful wills had been that of Elizabeth of Dean in Cheriton in the year 1727. Years ago we had tried to decipher gravestone inscriptions placed around the churchyard wall but with no success; as in most rural areas, the church had been locked, it was a Bank Holiday, and we hadn't liked to bother anyone.*
>
> *This time we were destined to be more fortunate. Not only did we notice and investigate the sign to Dean House and Dean Farm, but we met Mrs Ann Smart from the Manor who kindly unlocked the church for us and stayed to help us. Inside the church, on the north wall, is a precise and wonderfully executed plan of the churchyard with all the burial plots shown and numbered, with a beautiful little book showing all the burials listed in the records from about 1660, together with their plot numbers.*
>
> *This is a work of art, copied in perfect copperplate. We were able to find several family names and one new*

to us. We couldn't find Elizabeth's plot number, but it seems possible that she was buried in the crypt.

Ann Smart plays the organ for services and not only invited us to the village carol service but also directed us to the author of the burial plan, Ray Griffen. He was most welcoming and kindly took us back to the church for a closer examination of his handiwork. We felt privileged to be shown the beautiful oak pulpit which he had made to replace one which had not only been deteriorating but obscured the view of the sanctuary.

We were glad that we made the journey to the Kilmeston carol service on 20th December; we were made welcome and it was delightful to share in the nine lessons and carols in a church filled with people and music ...descants to well-known carols rising and soaring above us all.

St. Andrew's was built in 1772 on the foundations of what the Domesday survey noted as a chapel annexed to Cheriton, and it is thought to be of Saxon or Norman origin. In 1879 Kilmeston and Beauworth were separated from Cheriton and formed into a new parish in the gift of the Crown. The Beauworth-bound track which starts by Kilmeston's telephone box is known as Parson's Walk, although it is some time since it was used as such. It is also now some time - 23 years in fact - since the vicarage ceased to have a clerical occupant, subsequently becoming a private dwelling known as St Andrew's House. (There was, so one story goes, an alehouse on the site in pre-vicarage times - and thus filled no doubt with a different type of spirit!)

Kilmeston and Beauworth were split in 1972, with Kilmeston joining Bramdean and Hinton Ampner, and Beauworth returning to Cheriton. And while considering shifting parish boundary lines, it is interesting to note an entry from now seemingly remote Preshaw in Kilmeston's burial register for 1845: "Thomas Foster from The Holt, of this Parish"...

In his book on Hampshire, published 1905, the Reverend J. Charles Cox regrets the lack of remaining Norman features in St Andrew's and observes that "the church has lost almost all interest through severe restoration. It was first restored in 1865; in 1875 a new aisle was added and the church otherwise enlarged, and it underwent further treatment in 1898". The bell bears the date 1772, and the open bell-tower which replaced the original enclosed tower was designed by Bertram Chancellor of Winchester, commissioned and funded by Mr Heathcote of the Manor, and was built in 1911. Electric lighting arrived in Kilmeston in 1936, the church being wired up by Philip Dod from College Farm (now Gastons), and electric heaters replaced the coke stove in 1963. 1936 was also the year for a red curtain that had separated the vestry from the rest of the church to be replaced by an oak screen given by Mrs Mabel Vaughan-Morgan of the Manor, Mr Heathcote's elder daughter.

Music for services used to be provided by a harmonium, which - although no longer used - still remains in the church. The organ was presented in 1965 by Mrs Joy Colvin and her family, of Yew Tree Cottage, in memory of her late husband, Captain

Ivan Beale Colvin, Royal Navy. This organ had been taken out of Hook Parish Church and had been left lying in a builder's yard for some time before being rescued. The firm who installed it in St Andrew's fulfilled the mechanical and musical requirements, but it was Ray Griffen who hurriedly carried out the finishing touches, ready for its dedication: the old varnish had cracked badly, so he smartened up the surface; he also put in cupboards on either side, two swivelling mirrors and a raised wooden floor to meet the base of the new organ.

After the closure of the village school in 1926, the last schoolmistress - Miss Edwards - continued contributing to village life by playing the organ until well into her eighties, although the music apparently became "something of a hit and miss affair" towards the end of her life: with her failing eyesight and her hearing also deteriorating, Ray Griffen would have to flash a light when she was supposed to start playing; she would then sometimes play a bit and sometimes stop, when she could no longer see the music.

Annie Edwards was buried in the village churchyard in July 1970, aged 90. Her place at the organ was taken by Tilly Knight, formerly from Preshaw, whose brother - Ernest Dewey - had been butler at Kilmeston Manor and whose father had been first groom then chauffeur there.

The Manor news-cuttings album from the first two decades of this century contains an extract from *The Hampshire Chronicle and General Advertiser for the South and West of England* dated Saturday, 9th October, 1920, which gives a local illustration of the mores of the time:

> *KILMESTON - Double Wedding - An event of more than usual interest took place at the Parish Church at Kilmeston on Monday, with the double wedding of the eldest and second daughters of Mr and Mrs Dewey of The Cottage. Both parents of the brides are well-known*

7

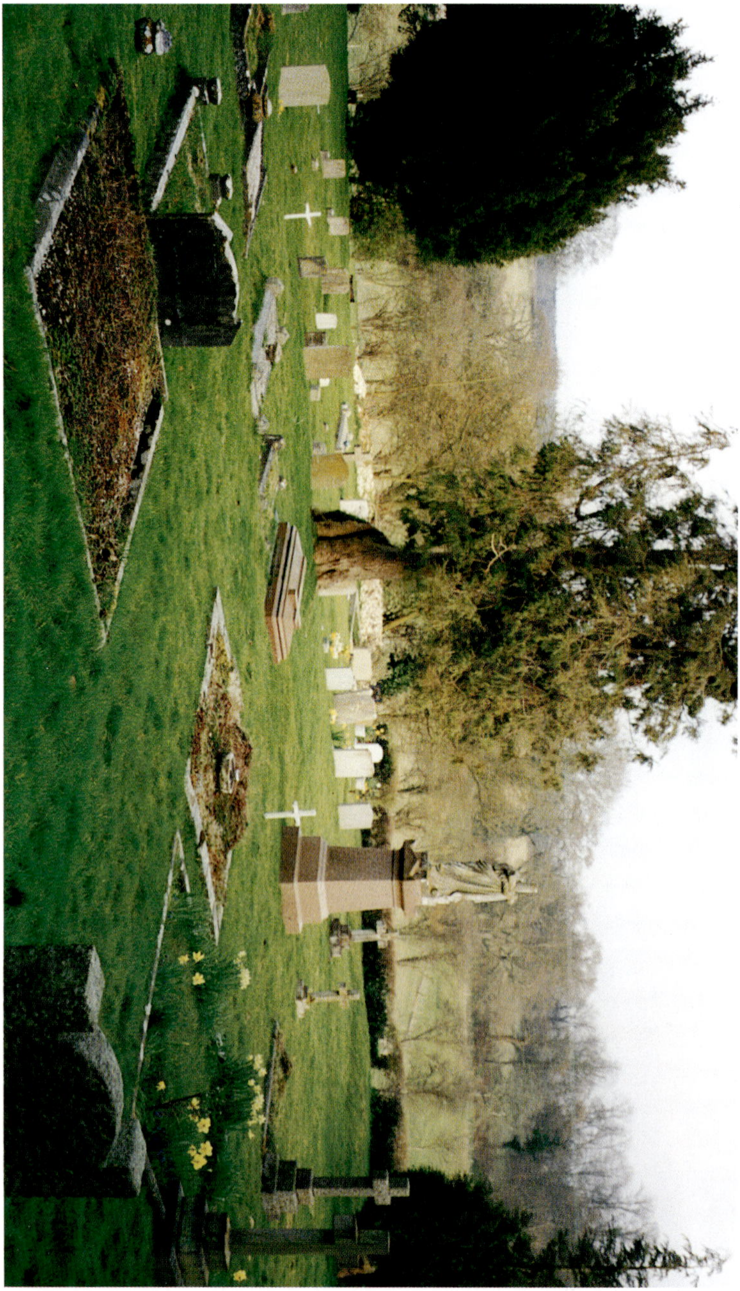

and respected in the district, Mr. Dewey having been in the service of the Heathcote family for many years. ...The Rev. C. Trimble officiated, the ceremony being fully choral. ...The choir was augmented by two cousins of the brides. [Tilly, the youngest daughter, was a bridesmaid.] By the kindness of Mr Heathcote, the reception was held in the billiard room of Kilmeston Manor. ...It may be mentioned that both the best men had served all through the war, Mr Newstead having distinguished himself by winning the Military Medal and the Serbian Medal. ...The bouquets of the brides and bridesmaids were made by Mr J. Childs (gardener to Mr Heathcote)...

There used to be a flourishing Sunday School. Miss Edwards presided over it from the organ, and Doris Abrahams was for several years the teacher. Ray Griffen, a boy at the time, remembers causing consternation by breaking the bell-rope just before Sunday School one morning and, since there was evensong that evening, an urgent repair had to be done.

Another, more recent, weekend drama that still sticks in village memories was in the Sixties, before the church roof was renewed, when a strong snowstorm blew vast amounts of snow in under the tiles. Fortunately water was discovered dripping through the ceiling on the Saturday, and a team of at least a dozen villagers was speedily drafted in to help save the church from flooding. A few gathered the snow in the roof into buckets and lowered these through a trap door to the others below - although apparently one bucketful accidentally landed on the vicar's bald head!

The church has excellent acoustics, as was recently demonstrated when The Elizabethan Singers of London and the English Performing Arts Ensemble gave concerts there. Generally, though, there is regrettably not much occasion these days for the acoustics to be tested.

From the old days of a church choir and weekly choir practice comes the story of a ghost, who was apparently seen in the road beside the churchyard. However, other reports suggest that this particular spectre was invented to persuade the choirboys to go straight home immediately after choir practice and not to dally with the choirgirls ... (Or maybe there really had been a sighting of Kilmeston's "Grey Lady"...)

Various areas have their own grey lady and their descriptions too can be various but, curiously, the totally independent descriptions of Kilmeston's grey lady all tally: she is apparently petite in stature, gentle of nature, has a very lined face, must have been pretty when young, and is dressed in a long bluish-grey cloak or robe. Sightings have been reported by the kissing-gate opposite the churchyard (more than once), in the Manor dining room once during the 1960s, and a couple of years ago in the garden outside the window of what was once the servants' hall at the Manor and is now the flat sitting room. The dining room sighting was by a young woman reportedly gifted with second sight (because she had been born with the bag of membranes over her head), and the garden sighting was by an American visitor, who, while playing the celtic harp one night, saw an old woman looking through the window and invited her in. The figure came straight through the wall and joined the young American, who strangely felt completely calm and even reassured by her presence. The apparition stayed briefly to listen and then vanished.

Mud Hut Lane, which lies behind the official source of the River Itchen, is also said to be haunted, in particular by an old sow and her piglets. "If you went along the lane a bit, you reached a part between two clumps of trees, where some folk got windy," to quote a local resident. Horses too would refuse to go along the track.

This lane is a continuation of the old coach road which runs down from the Winchester Road (or A272) along Sandy Lane and which is a short-cut still used today. The coach road used to cross the Kilmeston road, head east along Mud Hut Lane, then go under Hinton, across White Hill to Joan's Acre and join the main road near Brockwood. The old mud hut - possibly an old toll house - has long since disappeared, but the name remains.

Just to the west is the source of the River Itchen, most adequately described by Ralph Dutton (later to become Lord Sherborne) in his book *A Hampshire Manor*, which is a history of his home, Hinton House:

> At the base of the west end of the promontory lies the official source of the River Itchen - in a willow-filled dell on the east side of the lane to the village of Kilmeston. In the valley many springs make their contribution to the small trickle which emerges from the "official source", which, it must be owned, in a dry season hardly deserves its title, although in a wet season it projects a fine clear stream beneath the bridge carrying the Kilmeston lane.

*   *   *   *

The village school in Kilmeston was closed in 1926, having enjoyed a long run. A certain Dame Mary Sadler had bequeathed £100 at the beginning of the eighteenth century towards the establishment of a school; and after its closure, the interest from the money was then used for the Sunday School. (Dame Mary also bequeathed College Farm - now Gastons - towards the foundation of 16 lectureships in algebra within the University of Cambridge; these lectures started in 1710.) School was daily, with one schoolmistress and no more than 20 pupils. When it closed, the children went to Hinton and Cheriton, with "old Jack Mills" - a builder who lived in the cottage by the telephone box - transporting them in his lorry. The school building is now the village hall.

Village hall, formerly the school

An article about Kilmeston and its village life appeared in the *Hampshire Telegraph* on Thursday, 10th April, 1975. Journalist Reg Betts reported: 'On the other side of the green I met Mr George Kent, the 70-year-old retired postmaster and shopkeeper - and he frankly preferred the village as it was in the old days:

> *When I was young nearly everyone worked on local farms and there was a blacksmith's shop. We made our own amusement. There were whist drives and dances, a cricket club, and we used to have a club where we could play billiards. On pay nights the men used to walk back from the nearest pub singing - and sometimes scrapping. Don't get me wrong: Kilmeston is a nice, quiet little place, but for me it lacks the social atmosphere of the old days. ...I shut the post office down five years ago but kept the shop open as best I could until last March. At one time everyone relied on the village shop, but with so many having cars the trade went down.'*

The village dairy, run by George's parents, had previously been on the other side of the shop, and people would go down with their cans to collect milk. Around this time, judging from old photographs and backed up by recollections, the Old Post House was thatched. Prior to 1924, when the Anderson family came to Kilmeston, their cottage - Ivy Cottage - had been the village shop; the Kents' shop subsequently took over from it.

Main street through village, the village shop and post office on the left

The social club George Kent mentioned was in an old wooden hut called Tarry Point, situated near the church and roughly on the current site of the Waterstons' home, Rickaby. When the hut deteriorated and became dilapidated, the club moved first into a bungalow next to Dean Farm and then later - after the school closed - into the village schoolroom. Around this time there was a local character called "Old China" Elliott who used to get drunk at the club and would then hold mock church services on his way home through the village; sisters Jean Langrish and the late Mary Anderson recalled hearing him loudly chanting and preaching as he passed their cottage.

Doris Abrahams, who recently celebrated her 80th birthday, moved to Kilmeston from Somerset in 1925, when her father became gardener at College Farm. His employer, Mr Anthony Dod, used to play billiards with Mr Walter Heathcote at the Manor, and both men were great supporters of the club at the village hall. Doris remembers fortnightly whist drives at the club; delicious cakes from a popular cake shop opposite King Alfred's statue in Winchester made these evenings all the more memorable.

Billiards was far from being the only ball-game in Dod family life, tennis featuring in particular. Anthony Dod once won the mixed doubles tournament at Wimbledon with his sister, Lottie, the famed five-times Ladies' Champion. The Dod children also enjoyed the game, and when son Philip's car broke down in Southampton one morning, he ran over the hills back to Kilmeston in order not to miss tennis in the afternoon. (Philip is still fit and active and living in Berkshire.)

For some time after Tarry Point was abandoned, the small hut next to it continued in its use as the postman's hut. The postman came out from Alresford by bike early each morning, delivered his letters, and then made a meal for himself on a stove in the hut. Members of the village would join him there. He then emptied the local collection box in the afternoon and cycled back to Alresford. The remains of his hut now form a part of the Griffens' garden shed in Westwood View.

Margaret Griffen was born in Kilmeston and has lived here all her life, spending her early years in No. 3 Church Cottages; this has since been extended and renamed Pump Cottage. Her father was gardener to Mr C.G. Heathcote at the Manor, the present owner's great-grandfather. Margaret and her husband Ray (who came to Lower Kilmeston at the age of 4) remember wonderful children's Christmas parties at Dean House, which Sir Geoffrey and Lady Peto gave for many years around the late 1920s. There were more children in the village then, and more home-based entertainment, Philip Dod's shadow plays at College Farm (now Gastons) being a well-remembered example.

Another memory from that time, though perhaps less warmly treasured, is that of Sparky the Sweep. Sparky had only one eye and wore a black patch where the other had been, intriguing local children with the explanation that it had been gouged out by a glass stopper that had flown out of a "pop" (lemonade) bottle.

The most fondly cherished memory seems to be that of Nurse Owen, local nurse, midwife and friend to all. She would even tend the local gypsies on a small triangle of common ground on the hill just south of Down Farm. She is described as a "tall, thin, lovely person", who lived opposite the village green, went everywhere on her bicycle and on her retirement was given an Austin Seven motorcar by the district as a gesture of their appreciation.

When the Reverend R.J. Hitchcock left the parish, he passed on various useful pieces of information to the incoming vicar, the Reverend S.H.W. Lovett, particularly endorsing local praise for Nurse Owen, whose area covered not only Kilmeston but also

Beauworth, Cheriton, Preshaw and Hockley. He further added that, despite there not being enough boys in Kilmeston to run a separate (from Cheriton) scout troupe, "Miss Joan Dutton of Hinton Ampner is Captain of a (Girl Guide) Troupe to which many of the girls in this village belong: in fact they form nearly the entire company. From time to time they attend church here in a body with their colours". No doubt one of these occasions was Harvest Festival, when apparently the church would be filled to overflowing, and houses and farms - each with their staff - all attended.

The cricket recalled by George Kent used to take place in the field opposite Westwood View, on land owned by the Blakes of Manor Farm. The pitch was fenced in, to keep the cows at bay, and was mown by Margaret Griffen's father, using a horse-drawn mower supplied by Mrs Corbett of Hockley House. There was a small pavilion, though this was not large enough to accommodate the teams for the match teas: these were therefore held in the village hall and catered for by Mrs Anderson, mother of Jean Langrish and the late Mary Anderson.

Present-day village gatherings include the annual fête, summer barbecues and the monthly "First Fridays". To take the last first, these evenings - which were started on 2nd November, 1990, and take place in the village hall on the first Friday of each month - are the equivalent of a once-a-month pub. The premises are licensed and the evenings are run thoughtfully and efficiently by Graham Cresswell; they have done much to bring together members of the village and their news and views. (Do we hear the spirits of George Kent and "China Clay" muttering: "Plus ça change..."?)

The village hall with surrounding area is also the venue for highly successful summer barbecues, where the hot and seemingly tireless cooks cater for sometimes as many as 150 villagers and visitors.

But Kilmeston's big event is its annual summer fête, a traditional and herculean feat, to which punters come from far and wide. Despite fatigue at the end of the day, it is a rewarding experience and an opportunity for the whole village to pull together. During much of this century the fête took place in the Manor grounds, masterminded by the owner, Mrs Betty Smart; nowadays it is run by a committee, and the event has since 1988 been held at Dean House, thanks to the generosity of Philip Gwyn. The fête found fame in the *Field* magazine in July 1992, in an article written by Simon Cassey (now an ex-resident but fête chairman for the year in question). This was printed alongside a page of scene-capturing photographs taken by a *Field* photographer of the busy stalls and sideshows.

Playwright William Douglas-Home had also drafted an article about the fête, a copy of which he handed in to the Manor at the time. Sadly he died not long afterwards but his widow, Lady Dacre, has kindly allowed the following charming little vignette to be included here: [The treasurer is handed] "...the cash we have collected through a long and tiring afternoon spent seated at the entrance; though admittedly the afternoon is made less tiring by the offer and acceptance of a dram out of a flask which my nameless companion hides in the grass beside him - or, to be precise, he thinks he does."

Earlier, Dean House was the venue for other village activities, when the Peto family lived there: not only did they hold children's Christmas parties but they would sometimes open their garage as a cinema, showing black-and-white - and presumably silent - films. The Petos also built the squash court.

Another owner, Mr Hugo Money-Coutts, made substantial changes to Dean House, in particular removing servants' quarters. The Countess of Dundonald subsequently looked at the property but said it would not suit because there were not adequate staff quarters.

Mary Anderson, who was gardener at Dean House for many years, recalled an extraordinary and unexplained flood there in 1940. It had been a terrible winter, with freezing conditions and deep snow on the ground. Mary's father, who was himself gardener at Dean House at the time, was called out at 8 a.m. one Sunday as somebody in the house had gone downstairs first thing in the morning and found themselves in deep floodwater. The water filled the cellars, covered the ground floor and flowed out through the front door. A garden wall was even washed down. The cause was never established, but it was thought to be due to more than mere thawing. The owner, Mrs Steele, had been waiting for war evacuees to arrive, so had stocked the cellars with provisions, such as rice and other dried goods: these were of course all sodden through.

Dean House

During the earlier part of World War II Kilmeston was host to supply companies from the RASC (Royal Army Service Corps) and two or three artillery companies. Doris Abrahams remembers enjoying games of tennis with some of those billeted in the village, in particular on courts at the vicarage and at Dean House. Petrol supplies for the war were kept camouflaged and guarded day and night - in the Manor fields below the church.

Manor archives contain a list, compiled in February 1943, of the units based at Kilmeston Manor:

> *RASC Supply Column, O/C Major Boam, arrived 13 July 1940 and left 23 November 1940*
>
> *RASC Petrol Company, O/C Major Austin, arrived 24 November 1940 and left 30 November 1941*
>
> *R.A. Regiment of Medium Artillery, O/C Captain D. Moffat, arrived February 1942 and left 4 January 1943*
>
> *RAMC Field Ambulance, O/C Col. Kennedy, arrived 18 February 1943 and left 16 March 1943*
>
> *R.A. 187th Field Regiment (later 5th Regiment), O/C Lt. Col Crosse, M.C., arrived 19 April 1943*
>
> *R.A. 28th Search Light Regiment, O/C Major L. Jones, M.C., arrived 22 August 1943; also apparently in charge of a detachment from 28th (Essex) S.L. Regiment R.A.*

Mrs Joseie Ford, who recently retired as caretaker at Cheriton Primary School, was born in Kilmeston in the Manor Cottages by Parson's Walk; her father, Bertie Childs, was chauffeur at the Manor, and Joseie remembers her father putting large hampers into the Rolls - full of vegetables from the garden and groceries from the house - and taking them up to the London house during the period that Army units were in the Manor.

American troops were also based nearby, especially during the build-up to D-day, and those in Cheriton and Tichborne would sometimes be brought through Kilmeston on route marches. Bombs dropped on the hill past College Down Farm, and one buzzbomb - or "doodlebug" - fell in a field which is now part of

Blackthorn Nursery and opposite what was then called College Farm. A plane even came down in Bramdean, and the pilot baled out. Apropos of College Farm, there is also the story - still proffered by several in the village and which is open to conjecture - of the skylight: was a light really beamed through a skylight in the centre of the house, as a beacon for German bomber pilots...?

Shortly after the War, six council houses were built in the centre of the village; and in the early 1950s mains water pipes started to arrive, to replace the old and cumbersome method of bringing water up in buckets from garden wells. At this time the village hall was still owned by the PCC (Parochial Church Council); and children went to school in Beauworth if under 11 and to Perins School in Alresford if older.

There is still a school bus to Alresford from Kilmeston, but the nearest bus stop for the regular local service is at the crossroads on the A272.

* * * * *

In 1957 the Airey family bought the petrol station at the crossroads on the A272 and the shop, which was then on the opposite side of the road. Mr Airey ran the petrol station and his wife ran the shop, though when customers needing petrol rang the ship's bell on the forecourt, the Airey family would take it in turns to rush over the, even then, busy crossroads to serve the petrol. The petrol station at that time had a six-foot-square, wooden kiosk, two hand pumps and one electric pump, each of these dispensing a different brand of fuel (one BP, one Shell and one National Benzol); and it was open for four-and-a-half hours in the morning and three-and-a-half hours after lunch.

Continued success bred continued expansion, in terms of increased size of kiosk, of tanks and of opening hours. A new shop beside the filling station was finally built by Bill in 1987, to replace the old one across the road, the latter destined to become the antiques shop it now is. Bill's brother Tom had meanwhile carried out a similar expansion next to the old shop, taking over the storehouse and garage. At first he only repaired cars, but in the late Seventies he obtained a Saab franchise and then one for Subaru as well. He still enjoys not only fixing cars but racing them too, a trait he considers he inherited (his mother was once found by a Kilmeston resident trying to crawl out of an upturned fast car and magnificently swearing like a trooper before realising she had been recognised!)

*   *   *   *   *

Earlier this century fresh bread was still being delivered around Kilmeston from the local bakery, then on the site of the current antiques shop, Top Hat. There was a large oven at the back, where two daily baking sessions produced many different sorts of loaves. The bakery was run by Mr Pullinger, and his son Ernest remembers sampling the "tester" - a small roll which they as baker's children would have with butter for breakfast. The bakers used to burn "bunts", which were similar to faggots (bundles of wood). They burnt these out, scraped off the surplus ash, and then put the loaves in, having mixed the dough by hand. The bread was then delivered around the immediate locality by pony and trap. This pony was small and stubborn, with a mind of its own, and if it wanted to go only so far on the baker's round, more than mere coaxing was needed, and the delivery sometimes had to be postponed. The trap was an open-air vehicle, like a dogcart, and with two steps up; on wet days the bread was covered by a tarpaulin.

If the pony needed reshoeing, this was done in the village: Frank White, the blacksmith, would come up from Cheriton to use the forge at Kilmeston - now called Forge Cottage - and this building continued in its function as a forge until around 1930.

Main road through village, and Forge Cottage on right

*   *   *   *   *

Horses played a particularly dominant role in Kilmeston history during the eighteenth century when, in its early days, the Hampshire Hunt was also known as the Kilmeston Hunt. Thomas Ridge, owner and Lord of the Manor of Kilmeston, was a typical country squire of his time. The eldest son of George Ridge, a Portsmouth brewer, Thomas inherited Kilmeston Manor from his father, married his cousin Mary Ayles of Kilmeston at Portsea in 1767 and had 18 or 20 children (records vary). He took over the Kilmeston Hunt from his father, developing it into the Hampshire Hunt and maintaining it at his own expense until he eventually had to accept subscriptions towards the cost. The Prince of Wales, later to be George IV, stayed at the Manor for hunting; and the insignia of the "HH" (Hampshire Hunt) still includes the Prince of Wales's feathers. Reportedly 25th April, 1795 is the date when members of the Hunt first wore the Prince of Wales's feathers surmounting the monogram "HH" on their buttons.

On 15th December, 1785, the Prince married Mrs Maria Fitzherbert, a widow and quoted as "a Roman Catholic beauty". It was impossible for the Prince Regent to marry a Catholic legally, so he married her secretly, at her house in Park Street, Mayfair. He was 23 and she was 29. Mrs Fitzherbert's younger brother, John Smythe, Esq., who lived at Cheriton House, was one of the three members of Mrs Fitzherbert's family who attended the ceremony and witnessed the marriage certificate; he was also one of the original members of the Hampshire Hunt.

It was during one of his visits to Kilmeston Manor that "Prinny" etched on the window of what is now the kitchen - and was then presumably a reception room - four lines from Polonius's speech to Ophelia in Act II, Scene II, of Shakespeare's "Hamlet":

Doubt that the stars are fire;
Doubt that the sun doth move;
Doubt truth to be a liar;
But never doubt I love.

George R

These lines are clearly a dedication to Mrs Fitzherbert; and "doubt" is in fact spelt "dought". The kitchen window of the Manor was blown out by the stray buzzbomb that landed nearby during World War II, but the leaded panes were pieced together and most of the neatly written verse can still be seen.

A couple of the Ridge children followed their royal guest's example and scratched their names on the window of an upstairs room that was possibly then the nursery, though with less neat results... Various Ridge children are named in the church burial records; and, spanning the centuries, it is interesting to note that Olivia - now in her twenties and eldest of the current younger generation at the Manor - was the first child from the Manor to be baptised at Kilmeston since Caroline Ridge's baptism in 1793, 178 years earlier. It is also recorded in church records that Henry

Ridge, later to be Colonel Henry Ridge and hero of the Battle of Badajoz in the Peninsular War, was baptised in St Andrew's, Kilmeston, on 18th February, 1778; and that the Prince of Wales became godfather to the youngest Ridge son in 1790.

A wing was built onto the Manor at the north-east end to accommodate the Prince Regent and Mrs Fitzherbert - funded, so records claim, by George III. It comprised two reception rooms - over cellars - on the ground floor and two bedrooms above, with an intercommunicating double door between them.

The Prince of Wales married his cousin Caroline, a daughter of the Duke of Brunswick, at The Chapel Royal, St James's Palace, on 8th April, 1798.

In a letter sent to the Manor, Miss Edith Forward - who was a granddaughter of one of Thomas Ridge's 19 (she states) daughters - confirms the details about Prinny hunting with the Ridges and being entertained at the Manor. She adds that Thomas's wife Mary was an heiress, though Miss Forward comments that she had no idea where all the money went! The Manor archives also include a few letters written in 1952 by General John Hope of Preston Grange, Basingstoke (author of *Hunting in Hampshire*, published 1950) to Mrs Mabel Vaughan-Morgan (great-aunt of the current owner) and the following extracts provide entertaining glimpses into social life in the eighteenth century:

> *The Prince of Wales ...certainly knew Mr Ridge and asked him to bring his friends to Kempshott on February 11th, 1792. I think on this occasion, the field was graced by Lady Jersey and Lady Cunningham, Mesdames Stuart and Hodges all recruited. Mrs Fitzherbert did not hunt but expect would have enjoyed seeing either of the first named ladies return on a stretcher.*
>
> *In 1794 the Prince broke with Mrs Fitzherbert not, I fear, because of Prince Caroline of Brunswick whom he had the affrontery to bring to Kempshott for his*

The grass IS greener on the other side! (Spring lambs in the Manor orchard, the Church Cottages and Manor Cottages in the background.)

Kilmeston Manor

honeymoon, but because he had fallen victim to the mature charm of Lady Jersey. He did not again live with Mrs Fitzherbert till 1799. I wonder that noble woman could ever have put up with such a disreputable husband.

Squire Thomas Ridge died on 3rd February, 1801, and was buried at Kilmeston, "in the churchyard that gently slopes to the Manor Field below". A memorial plaque on the wall inside the church bears the following inscription:

*Near this Place are deposited the Remains of
THOMAS RIDGE, Esq., Lord of the Manor of
Kilmeston.*

*A Steady Friend
And liberal Master
In private Life.
An inflexible Patriot
An upright Magistrate
In Public.*

*He departed this Life the third day of
February 1801. In the 64th Year of his
Age.
Beloved, revered and deeply lamented by his
affectionate Widow.
And by his numerous Family.*

Thomas Ridge's characteristics quoted above are echoed by the Reverend C. Powlett in *Songs from the Hampshire Hunt Club*: "a man without guile; the truth you might read in his eyes". And the words on the plaque were re-read most recently by some of his "numerous family" in 1991, when Rupert and Blanche Ridge came over from Bristol on a surprise visit with their four children - the eldest being called Thomas - to see both church and Manor.

* * * * *

The latter was advertised in The Times on Friday, 12th June, 1801, as follows:

> *Hampshire, Mansion House, Manor and Farms. A valuable and very desirable Freehold Estate, Comprising the Manor of Kilmiston, with a capital Mansion House, Offices, large walled garden, farmyard with all useful buildings, and upwards of 600 acres of excellent arable, meadow, pasture and woodland, with 11 neat brick messuages and tenements, and gardens, all lying perfectly compact, together with an estimated equivalent of upwards of 200 acres of down pasture adjoining, pleasantly and healthfully situated at Kilmiston in a fine sporting country.*

Manor records confirm that there were about 1,000 acres attached to the house at this time, though many of these presumably went southwards when Mr George Long from Preshaw subsequently bought the property but sold the house soon afterwards.

Kilmeston Manor

Twenty years later William Cobbett noted in his *Rural Rides:* "A bridle road over some fields and through a coppice took me to Kilmston, formerly a large village, but now mouldered into two farms and a few miserable tumble-down houses for the labourers. Here is a house, that was formerly the residence of the landlord of the place, but is now occupied by one of the farmers. ...A little to our right, as we came along, we left the village of Kilmston, where Squire Graeme once lived".

This Squire Graeme referred to by Cobbett was Charles Graeme of Dean House and Honorary Secretary of the Hampshire Hunt for many years. He was buried in Kilmeston churchyard in 1833 and a plaque on the wall inside the church commemorates both him and his wife.

Cobbett goes on: "Here too lived Squire Ridge, a famous foxhunter, at a great mansion, now used as a farmhouse." Cobbett also mentions that Mr Long's steward, a Mr Gunner, attorney at Bishop's Waltham and son-in-law of Squire Ridge, "kindly furnished some of these particulars".

For those who enjoy figures, records claim that in 1839 the parish of Kilmeston contained 1,640 acres, of which 114 were pasture, 185 down, 128 woods and coppices, 26 public and private roads, and the remaining 1,187 arable. The whole of the parish had been enclosed, under an act of parliament, in 1805, the original copy of this act being recently moved from the Manor to the new County Records Office in Winchester.

On 7th June, 1893, a Mrs Beaufort bought the Manor and made substantial changes. Her researches showed that the house had once been much larger and that there had been another wing on the side nearest the church; also that there had been a brewhouse adjoining the dairy (both now forming the Manor flat). Among the alterations, Mrs Beaufort requested a new cupboard in what had been a downstairs reception room but which she wished to have as a large central hall, reaching up to the second storey. She asked the workmen to knock out the panelling, whereupon a "priest's hole" was revealed, containing a knight in armour. As the incredulous workmen watched, the knight's body dissolved into dust, leaving only his metal accoutrements whole: the air had been so dry and pure inside the hiding place, that the knight had remained perfectly preserved until fresh air was admitted.

The so-called "priest's hole" was a legacy from the time shortly after the Reformation when an attempt to reform the Roman Catholic Church had resulted in the establishment and ultimate supremacy of the Protestant Churches. Many old Catholic families continued to celebrate Mass, but they had to have a safe, secret place in which they could hide the priest if soldiers should chance to come by to check on them.

This particular fugitive cavalier had apparently sought sanctuary after being wounded in the nearby Battle of Cheriton on Friday, 29th March, 1644, when the Royalists were severely beaten by the Roundheads.

Telford Varley's account of the battle is one of the clearest, stating that:

> ...*on the issue hung the supremacy of Royalist or Roundhead in the south-eastern counties. The Roundhead base was Farnham, while Winchester and Basing were strongly held for the Royalists, and Lord Hopton, the Royalist commander's object was to prevent the advance of Waller coming up from Petersfield. As the foe drew near, Hopton advanced his outposts. He had seized Alresford and pushed his men out eastward along the ridge between Tichborne and East Tisted, thus commanding the roads along which Waller must pass. If Hopton could but hold his ground, Waller was checkmated.*

The actual battle commenced at eight in the morning. Each army had a strong position. Waller held the high ground near Cheriton village, with Cheriton Wood and detached hedges in the hollow between them and the Royalists.

The wood was an important strategic point. For hours in the hollow the contest raged fiercely; the Royalists steadily drove back the enemy until, advancing too far, they came under the fire from Waller's men entrenched and sheltered beneath the hedges. This was the crisis of the day, and Waller's men, seeing them waver, attacked in turn. According to tradition Lamborough (locally sometimes "Lamberry" or "Lambly") Lane ran with blood, and the slaughter was very heavy - 900 on the Parliament side, 1,400 on the Royalist.

It would seem that the family at the Manor were either taken away by Cromwell's men or fled and that there was nobody left who knew how to release the cavalier, if indeed anyone remaining knew he was there. Or maybe answers lie in a walled-up cellar beneath the old centre of the house, where metal detectors indicate there to be much iron... There is also the story of an underground passage from the Manor in the direction of Hinton Ampner to Dog-Kennel Wood - just to the north-east of College Farm - where the horses were kept for a quick retreat. But, whatever happened, the unlucky cavalier remained *in situ* for the next 250 years.

* * * * *

Mrs Beaufort never actually lived at Kilmeston Manor and sold it in March 1895 to Francis Wynde Cuthbert Beade, Esq., who was connected both with the Long family and the Dutton family. (Sir I. Beade had married Jane, daughter of Sir R. Dutton of Sherborne.) The two oak-panelled reception rooms were then made into one large room, other internal improvements were carried out, greenhouses were built, and the gardens received much attention.

In August 1899 Mr Beade sold the property to Mrs Anna Stirling, and three years later it was bought by Charles Gilbert Heathcote, great-grandfather of the present owner.

C.G.H. - as he is known to the family - was the younger son of John Moyer Heathcote of Conington Castle, Huntingdonshire, and both men were pupils of Peter De Wint, the prominent nineteenth-century British watercolour artist; both were also outstanding tennis players. C.G.H. achieved a First Class Classical Tripos at Cambridge and was called to the Bar at the Inner Temple. In 1869 he married The Hon Lucy Edith Wrottesley, and they had one son, Walter, and two daughters: Isobel, later to be Mrs Broke, and Mabel, later to be Mrs Vaughan-Morgan. These last two women are still remembered by some in the village today.

It was C.G.H.'s father who, in the autumn of 1874, invented the modern design of tennis ball cover. Hitherto the balls had firstly not been of uniform size and secondly, being uncovered, "used to bound in most erratic fashion, according to their age, shape and dimensions" (see *The Badminton Library*). C.G.H.'s daughter - the present owner's grandmother - would relate how her aunts would spend many hours stitching covers onto rubber balls for their tennis-playing menfolk. These covers were made of material taken at first from their warm flannel petticoats and subsequently led to the balls themselves being of a more uniform size, to fit the new cloth covers.

In a letter to the *Field, The Country Gentleman's Newspaper* of 5th December, 1874, J.M. Heathcote wrote from C.G.H.'s Brighton home:

> *...I will take this opportunity of making known to your readers some innovations that I have adopted, and which have been approved by all who have tried them. I use indiarubber balls, about two-and-a-half inches in diameter, covered with white flannel.*

And he goes on to recommend the uses of these balls, the best "bats" to use with them and which size of court to adopt; he also offers to help draw up a guideline for rules.

For some years C.G.H. was Lawn Tennis Amateur Champion, and he was one of the founder members of the All England Lawn Tennis Club. Tom Todd in *The Tennis Players* writes that the year 1877 was to "determine whether the game was... to take its place permanently among recognised English sports". The editor of the *Field* at that time was also the honorary secretary of the All England Croquet Club and "in April 1877 the committee of that club decided on a bold step and changed the name of the club to incorporate the name of the new game. It was determined to establish the club as the leading lawn tennis club as well as the leading croquet club. ...It was agreed in June 1877 ...to establish the first lawn tennis championships. ...The All England Club appointed a subcommittee consisting of ...and C.G. Heathcote to draw up rules for the proposed championship meeting". The latter subsequently wrote the section on Lawn Tennis in *The Badminton Library*.

C.G.H. held the post of Stipendiary Magistrate at Brighton for 18 years before his retirement, whereupon he came to live at Kilmeston. Here he died, eleven years later, and in a newspaper obituary was described as "a thoroughly accomplished gentleman, and a humane and charitable man of high culture, of firm character, of strong artistic feeling and energy, having a capacity for polished humour, and possessed of a most warm and generous heart".

He is buried, with other members of his family, in Kilmeston churchyard; and there is a commemorative brass plaque on a wall inside the church, erected by his children.

C.G.H's widow continued living at Kilmeston Manor until her own death in 1918, when the house passed to their son, Walter; and then in 1936 to Walter's elder sister Mabel, wife of Gwyn Vaughan-Morgan. Mr Vaughan-Morgan carried out various renovations and additions to the house and died in May 1945. Mabel continued to live at Kilmeston during the summer months until 1952, when she moved in permanently with her widowed sister, Isobel Lucy Broke. In January 1955, the house and estate were inherited by Mrs Elizabeth Smart, daughter of Isobel and mother of the current owner.

Few other houses in the area are still owned and occupied by the same family, several generations on. In Kilmeston itself, there has been much change...

Dean House has had various owners during this century. Manor Farm stopped being a farm in 1948 when the farmer and his wife, Mr and Mrs Blake, emigrated to Canada and Admiral and Mrs Graham moved into the house, the farmland being bought by John Corbett (son of Mrs Corbett of Hockley House - who lent the pony-driven mower for Kilmeston's cricket pitch).

College Farm underwent a name-change to Gastons as well as extensive alterations around the latter part of the 1940s, when owned by the Leventhorpe family; the name "Gastons" derives from Gastons Field, which adjoined the house and where Midsummer's Eve revelries were annually held and villagers would receive free beer and buns.

Stanmore House became separated from its stables: these were built by the Mahoney family - who then lived at Stanmore - and formed part of a new estate when the Mahoneys built and moved into Derry House around 1970. Since then there has been very little construction in Kilmeston, but six new houses are shortly to be built in the centre of the village, on the site of a grain dryer and old farm buildings that originally belonged to Manor Farm.

A comparatively recent arrival, Blackthorn Nursery, has firmly made its mark in the village and has found fame nationwide, not least among the followers and fans of rare flora. It was started in 1983, when an area nicknamed "The New Forest" and the field behind it were bought from the Manor estate. The nursery has thrived, and its owners - Robbie and Sue White - have won not only prizes in London but also acclaim from journalists both at home and abroad.

*   *   *   *   *

Village postbox and bus shelter; The Old Post House in the background

The village bus shelter, which now serves also as a newspaper delivery point and a notice board, was erected by Admiral Kemmis Betty, who lived in Yew Tree Cottage on the other side of the village green. Apropos of yew trees, it is interesting to note that the yew is sometimes termed "the Hampshire weed", being so much in evidence around here as to be considered indigenous to the county; and Kilmeston surely produces its fair share, both of trees and of hedges. The former were originally planted on the Downs, to mark the path across an otherwise trackless waste.

Historic hedges likewise abound in and around Kilmeston: the old Anglo-Saxon mixes of thorn (of all types), hazel, oak, ash and - occasionally - walnut still endure in many fields. Not only is the blend attractive to look at but it creates an excellent shelter for horses and requires little more than an occasional trim in the way of maintenance.

Still regularly used, by keen walkers and dog-owners in the main, a public footpath passes through the village. However walks around the core of the village sadly no longer contain the attraction of the village duckpond, which was on the road edge of the garden of Pond Cottage and provided - until not so long ago - a tangible goal for walks with young children.

A few yards to the west of the site of the old duck-pond lies a small piece of wood on the southern roadside bank that stirs the curiosity of passers-by: a memorial tablet commemorates the private pack of drag hounds that were kept by Mr Walpole of Dean House. Apparently he was of German extraction and had to return to Germany prior to World War I; so he arranged for the hounds to be put down after his departure. The original memorial tablet was stolen but was so missed that a new one was made by Ray Griffen and erected in 1994.

*   *   *   *   *

Many traditional elements of English villages have disappeared over the years, some of this passing being due to social and economic changes and pressures. However, the average village today still has a distinct character reflecting its inhabitants' current way of life.

In medieval times the manor was not only a lord's residence but also the district over which he had jurisdiction. The medieval ancestors of the county squires were knights who had acquired land in return for military service; then in peacetime they gradually became country gentlemen, improving their lands and properties and devoting themselves to local administration.

Their latter-day survivors are depicted benignly by The Rt Hon The Lord Deedes, MC, in an article in the *Field* in January 1994: "Our literature is rich in portraits of the English squire of the 19th and 20th centuries. He has come down to us mainly as a figure who rode, drank, lived hard and indulged in certain eccentricities." Lord Deedes continues: "Today's squire drinks less, is less autocratic and less dotty than some of his predecessors, but he inherits to the full a deep love of the countryside and all its recreations."

From the late nineteenth century onwards the demise of the power and influence of the squirearchy came gradually but inevitably in the wake of the import of cheap grain from abroad, and the Industrial Revolution offered bosses and workers alike a wider array of jobs.

The old form of village life, which focused on the activity of farming, is indeed gone. Most village-dwellers these days commute to work in a town and return to the village to relax; however they generally appreciate being part of a community and will consequently support and strive to maintain the traditional heart of the village as found in church, shop, school or village hall.

During the hibernatory months Kilmeston may appear to be comatose, but bring in the windsurfing season and the main (coast-bound) thoroughfare can resemble a racetrack; a village barbecue, a funeral or a fund-raising event can also achieve a transformation.

Straggling thinly as it does, Kilmeston is hardly the archetype of a classic English village and has few of the characteristics associated with standard village settings as conjured up by writers of fiction. Yet, despite being little more than a hamlet and having no regular public transport, no nearby railway station, no mains drainage, no mains gas, no cable TV, no pub within the village (the *Jolly Farmer* on the A272 is Kilmeston's most local "local", yet it lies just outside the parish boundary), no village shop, and no cinema nearer than half-an-hour by car, Kilmeston is no extinct species. It is not cowed by change or modernisation, the success of its survival appearing to lie in gradual evolution and gentle readjustment. If William Cobbett were to ride this way once again, he would surely be favourably impressed not only by Kilmeston's improved appearance but also by its sturdy survival qualities.

"The old order changeth," Tennyson said, "yielding place to new": a new century beckons, and this Kilmeston will - as ever - take in its unhurried and timeless stride.

* * * * *

BIBLIOGRAPHY INCLUDES:

The Concise Oxford Dictionary of English Place-names
AA Illustrated Guide to Britain
Shell Book of English Villages
Sketches of Hampshire - by John Duthy (first published 1839)
Hampshire - by Telford Varley
The Boys Own Paper (1889)
A Hampshire Manor - by Ralph Dutton
The Victoria History of Hampshire
St. Wilfrid's Parish Magazine, Cowplain (Sonia Passingham)
THE FIELD Magazine
Mrs Carden's scrapbook of 1952
The Badminton Library
The Tennis Players - by Tom Todd
HAMPSHIRE - by J. Charles Cox
Kilmeston Manor archives, scrapbooks, etc.